Windows 8  Programming Genius: 7 Easy Steps To Master Windows 8 Apps In 30 Days

Learning How to Use Windows 8 Efficiently

By: Jason Scotts

TABLE OF CONTENTS

Publishers Notes..3

Dedication 4

Chapter 1- Windows 8- What is it All About?...........................5

Chapter 2- Understanding How Files, Apps & Programs Work.......9

Chapter 3- Using the Internet with Windows 8....................13

Chapter 4- How to Make Changes to Windows 8- Doing
Customizations & Upgrades..17

Chapter 5- Windows – How Storage Works- The Options.............21

Chapter 6- How to Create & Edit Movies, Photos and Music...........25

Chapter 7- How to Find Lost Files in Windows 8 31

Chapter 8- The Art of Printing from Windows 8...................35

About The Author..39

Jason Scotts

PUBLISHERS NOTES

Disclaimer

This publication is intended to provide helpful and informative material. It is not intended to diagnose, treat, cure, or prevent any health problem or condition, nor is intended to replace the advice of a physician. No action should be taken solely on the contents of this book. Always consult your physician or qualified health-care professional on any matters regarding your health and before adopting any suggestions in this book or drawing inferences from it.

The author and publisher specifically disclaim all responsibility for any liability, loss or risk, personal or otherwise, which is incurred as a consequence, directly or indirectly, from the use or application of any contents of this book.

Any and all product names referenced within this book are the trademarks of their respective owners. None of these owners have sponsored, authorized, endorsed, or approved this book.

Always read all information provided by the manufacturers' product labels before using their products. The author and publisher are not responsible for claims made by manufacturers.

© **2013**

Manufactured in the United States of America

DEDICATION

This book is dedicated to my parents. They are my number one fans and supporters.

CHAPTER 1- WINDOWS 8- WHAT IS IT ALL ABOUT?

Microsoft has been offering operating systems for computer systems for the better part of 25 years now. However, the majority of these years, only two real operating systems held longevity for consumers: Windows 95 and Windows XP. These two operating systems changed the game in terms of what an individual could do on a computer, without the assistance of DOS right there, in your face.

After Windows XP, which came out right after the turn of the century, many of the follow up operating systems did not make the desired impact Microsoft would have wanted. This is where the new Windows 8 looks to change that, and the game, once again. Windows 8 is heavily based on touch screen devices and is actually based on the mobile operating system used for its lineup of mobile phones. With this in mind, there are some new features and services offered by Windows 8 that are designed to improve the way the operating system functions and all of the options you are able to perform on it.

New Tile Look

Windows 8, similar to what came about first in Windows 7, has done away with the old "Start' screen and menu. While it is still possible to access the start menu through a few gestures, you are greeted with a "Tile" look. The tiles appear on the screen and are different applications and programs you can easily access, all of them updating in real time. This way, you can have a Facebook tile, weather tile, word processor tile and others, all of which are updated, when necessary. This way, you can easily select the application or program you want to run by simply placing your finger to the tile on the touch screen display, or by clicking on the display button with your computer mouse. Either way, you have far greater access to the programs, and best of all, there is no slowdown in performance.

With so many programs running in real time, Windows has managed to avoid any lag of performance, which might have been a problem in other operating systems previously released from Microsoft. This way, you can have dozens of different applications updating in real time, and you don't have to worry about these at all slowing down the computer system.

Lock Screen

If you have been using mobile Smartphones for a while, you know what the lock screen is all about. The Windows 8 lock screen is similar, as it provides you some useful information, all without having to wake up the computer and return to the Tile display. You can select a different image if you desire to be the background, or you can have it rotate between pictures saved on the computer and those you took yourself. From there, the lock screen displays the time, weather temperature, if you have any new messages through Facebook or your email, and other general information you might want to know first thing. When you wake up your computer and return to the Tile screen, you know what to look for and if you have any messages you need to check. This way, it should prove rather helpful in locating your information, without you having to dig around for it and try to find it.

Desktop

If you are not sure about the Tile look of the new Windows 8 operating system, do not worry, because there is still the traditional desktop look, which should make you feel a bit more comfortable. When you go to the taskbar, which can still be found in the lower, left corner of the desktop, you can access the desktop view, which is going to run in a similar manor as the older, Windows OS you are used to. There are new buttons and offerings, so there are still some steps you need to inspect in order to understand how it works, but this should give you all of the necessary service and access you might require.

Integrated Apps

Windows has always boasted a large lineup of programs, but now you are able to run simple applications as well. Applications are basically streamlined programs that take up less RAM and are easier to run, due to the creation and design of the apps. You can download and install these applications onto your computer, and many of these work on the Tile screen. You can select the tiles and receive a small window of the application, or you can go further into the app and have it take up the entire screen. This way, no matter how you want to enjoy your application, you are going to receive all of this information and performance options right in front of you, using the new Windows 8 application design.

You can also pin your favorite applications, so you are never stuck with specific apps in the Tile menu. If you find you do not like some of these tiles on your screen, you can quickly and easily remove them. You can also alter the size of the app tile screens, so if one is more important than another, you can easily make it larger and more noticeable, which should help you out even further. All of this is designed to be easier for you to navigate and access things, and although there is a bit of a learning curve, you shouldn't have much of an issue with it in the long run.

There are many new features in the Windows 8 operating system, all of which are designed to change the way you interact with your computer system. Because of this, you are going to find that it is rather easy to access information and you might find that you are going to have to experiment at first but ultimately, it is an excellent experience and something that you are going to enjoy, especially if you have a touch screen based computer that is able to run your favorite programs.

CHAPTER 2- UNDERSTANDING HOW FILES, APPS & PROGRAMS WORK

Windows 8 has many advanced features to make file management, applications, and programs work better than the highly successful Windows 7. One of the useful advances is in the file management system called the File Explorer. It is a remodeled version of Explorer.

How Do Files Work in Windows 8? For the most part, there is a significant similarity with Windows 7 and a greater distance from Windows XP. Introduced after Windows XP, the ribbon feature is the main point of departure. It is the interface feature users find to be most-unlike Windows XP.

A change in Windows 8 is the new File Explorer. It contains new and reshaped features. One older feature is the ability quickly to return to the main or preceding file. As one searches files from a large folder to large files to smaller files, one must often retrace a step and go up to the previous level. The 'up' function has become the up-button. Positioned between back and forward arrows, it gives the user the required range of search controls to navigate through a file tree.

Another new feature is a new ribbon function that works according to the file or folder one selects. As one selects a folder, group of files, or individual file, the available options flash into view from the background. Keyed to the selection, they provide instant controls without redirecting one's movements and attention to a side panel. Set in the context of the user's actions, these options add choices to the constant items on the controls ribbon. The benefits of this feature are immense. There are hundreds of commands associated with the file or folder types. Arranged in a searchable hierarchy, that, however, requires a stop and search to gain access to them. This context feature brings many functions to the user's fingertips without loss of place or diversion from the task- at-hand.

The ribbon in the File Explorer has defined parts. The structure revolves around four broad functions: File Menu, Home, Share, and View. These parts work together to give the user several directions of controls and most of the necessary commands for locating items. The file menu has a help button and some basic commands such as command prompt and a new window. As in other parts of File Explorer, a context pane opens to list of relevant options.

The Home Tab provides the main-file commands that one needs to navigate, locate, open, and organize files. One can delete files; move or copy files, and rename files. It has an Easy Access command that pins an item to the start menu so that one can keep it in a place convenient to the task. There is an advanced feature called File History that can be set to keep a copy of an original file in a safe place. When it detects changes, the program can automatically send a copy of the file to a designated file, back-up, or outside location. This may prove to be a savior for an accidental or error in file management.

There are 'favorite' and 'library' options for files as well as 'open' and 'edit' commands. The 'select' function allows one to make commands for individual files or groups of files. The home tab is a constant feature on the ribbon.

The Share tab is a central point for all of the sharing functions. One can set access, restrict changes, send to Zip, print, fax, or burn to a disc. The addressable sharing options can be set to a group or to specific individual users. Restrictions can be set in the security section, to limit permissions.

The View tab controls the file display features. There are commands that determine the style and locations for viewing files such as details pane and preview panes. There are show and hide options which are vital for security and operations. Inadvertent deletions or changes to certain files can affect the entire system.

How do apps work in Windows 8? With any new system, there is a need to assess whether the software will run well. For one's existing software, especially older software, one must assess compatibility. The first tool in a logical sequence for converting to Windows 8 is the Windows 8 Upgrade Assistant. This feature of Windows 8 preparation gives the user a report, which describes steps, needed to adjust the software to the new OS environment. One can keep the report for post-installation use.

The report identifies issues and offers suggestions. Windows offers post-installation help for applications that need adjustment or new programming, such as drivers or updates. If so directed, one can assess these items in the Action Center. The next is the Windows Compatibility Center that provided details on difficulties and resolutions for compatibility. The center provides info on approximately one thousand applications and devices, and access to a community response resource. The communities have the advantage of sharing experiences with users of comparable applications and computers.

Compatibility modes are another powerful tool in the effort to make applications run on Windows8. This function converts the system to an earlier version such as Windows 7 or Windows XP. This tool is also usable with troubleshooter options. These evaluations may recommend compatibility-modes to solve problems that one might encounter.

How Do Programs Work in Windows 8? New programs designed to run with Windows 8 typically do not experience compatibility difficulties. Engineered with the features of this new system, and optimized for compatibility, one encounters few difficulties in operating them. In a similar way to applications and devices, the older items often have the greater difficulty. Compatibility modes are usually the test; if the program will not run in the older modes, then it is probably time to replace it.

Largely determined by the advances in related hardware and software, programs have a limited useful life. Computer makers add features, improve speeds, and provide capacity for more complex operations than earlier machines. Software moves in the same directions. Software advances require more memory, faster computing speeds, and a greater workload on data processing. Graphics and interactive features in software cause substantial leaps forward in the amount and types of work computers can do. Software is the vehicle for the advances, and at some point, the newer equipment will no longer adapt to older software.

CHAPTER 3- USING THE INTERNET WITH WINDOWS 8

Windows 8 is highly anticipated but can be difficult to get used to. Forget what all the other web browsers looked like, this one is vastly different. Everything has been moved and shifted for a more sleek and sophisticated internet experience. Completed in this package are two internet suits, both that bear the name of Internet Explorer, the most popular browser around. The first one can be found on the window start screen and the second one is found on the one is on the desktop.

It is confusing to some because although the web browsers are different, they are very similar. Because of this reason they share the browsing information and history, cookies, saved passwords and temporary files. If the user was to delete one or all of these items from one of the browsers, it would automatically delete them from the other browser as well. So while they are different, they are the same, make sense?

The browser from the start screen will show things only in full screen view. It has some limitations, and there is no way to place two internet sites side by side to compare them. If a person wants to open the internet explorer from the start screen and have quicker browsing opportunities, they just need to simply click the tile. The browser will open and fill in the screen with the homepage that is used on the desktop browser. Easy access is what the design of Microsoft Windows 8 is all about.

There are commands that allow a person to get a different screen with hidden menus. The mouse can be right clicked in any portion of the web page that is blank. Or to use the keyboard, press the Window button plus the Z button at the same time. Those using a touch screen computer can take their finger and slide the screen up and it will reveal the hidden menu. These menus hold a variety of items, including the last visited sites. To get to another area, simply click the selected tile and it will direct to that screen. By closing or hitting the X on the screen, it will remove them from the browsing history. By clicking the + icon in the right hand corner of the screen, it will allow a blank web browser page to appear.

By clicking the tab and tools option, it brings another drop down menu that has two options. They are new and private tab and closed tabs. To visit a website privately that doesn't leave a history in the browser memory, click the private tab. When the privacy button is turned on, the browser will forget the computer visited this area. To clear all previously viewed sites that appear in the browser thumbnail, simply click on the closed tab. On the bottom left hand corner of the screen is an arrow. By clicking this arrow, it will allow the user to go back to the previously viewed page.

The bottom of the hidden menus has a bar where a web-page address or a subject can be found. If typing a specific item for searching, it will check the internet and bring the best matches. By clicking inside the address bar, it will give a list of the most frequently visited sites. It will also display any sites that have been pinned to the start screen. If there are sites that a person visits frequently, they can be utilized in this section. While it takes only a few minutes to type in an address, why would anyone want to do that if they don't have to?

The refresh button is often used for those who frequent news sites. It gives up to date information with the touch of the button. Since some sites, like news channels, change often, this button comes in handy. In the right hand bottom corner is also a stick pin icon, this is called pin to start. Also online auction sites love this button, as the prices are constantly changing with bidding wars. Refresh is a great tool and now it is easy to locate. When you find something on a webpage you like and want to revisit, you can pin it. It will add the page you want to the start screen as a tile. This allows quick access for any return visits.

The third icon on the bottom right hand corner is a page tool. It has two options find on page and view on the desktop. The find on page tool allows you to find information on the specific page that is needed. The view on the desktop allows a person to view that information on the desktop in a larger screen. This is handy if the start screen's browser is not displaying something correctly. There is a third option under this icon that is grayed out, but it only offers this icon if there is an app for direct access.

When a person needs more power than the simple start screen browser has to offer, the desktop version of Windows 8 explorer usually suffices. To find this version, click the start screen's desk top tile. When this page appears, it is easy to see the internet explorer's icon in the bottom of the left hand screen. The desk top version of internet explorer provides the same options as past versions. It allows one to move from page to page by clicking links, typing a web address in the address bar and or using the systems amazing navigation buttons.

To go back to the homepage, simply right click the home button. The favorites icon in the top right hand corner, allows a person to add their favorite screens for easy access. The search box links the person to Google's vast search engine network for finding information fast. Some have reported that other browsers won't work with Windows 8. As with anything new, there are still some bugs that are being worked out.

CHAPTER 4- HOW TO MAKE CHANGES TO WINDOWS 8- DOING CUSTOMIZATIONS & UPGRADES

Advancements in technology have led to the development and creation of major technological innovations. From Smartphones to tablets to laptops and computers, we are now afforded the opportunity to complete school or business related tasks anywhere. Today, computers and laptops come with the Windows 8 operating system. Therefore, knowledge about customizations and upgrades is essential in assessing all the advantages granted to Window 8 users.

Do you fear the use of technological devices such as computers because you're not experienced with its use? Millions of older persons are so set in their ways that they do not even attempt to use computers or laptops. Older people would rather stick to the older methods they were raised on instead of learning the newer modern way of doing things with technology. That's absolutely fine. It is normal to want to preserve your natural way of doing things. However, in today's world you need to make some changes and accommodations.

Although it is great to know how to do things without the use of technology, it is even better to learn multiple ways of doing things. This is essential especially when one method is not available because you will be able to utilize another approach in which you're already knowledgeable about.

You do not have to go out become a computer geek and learn every little thing about computers. However, you should know the basics. You should know how to use programs such as Microsoft

Word, be able to browse the web, and you should also be familiar with the Windows 8 operating system.

Are you already computer savvy? Great, you're a step ahead of everyone else. You may or may not be familiar with the programs offered by the Windows 8 operating system. If you happen to have a Windows 8 operating system you should take the time to browse through the various programs which they offer and try a few of them. Let's take a closer more in-depth look at the Windows 8 operating system.

Are you having trouble navigating through the Windows 8 system? No need to worry. There are computer technicians, networking specialists, as well as tech support specialist available to answer any of your questions which may arise.

Want to learn how to customize the lock screen on Windows 8? The Windows 8 lock screen is not just a background or image it consists of widgets called lock screen apps that display quick notifications. These widgets enable you to view and access information including emails, instant messages, updates from social media websites, and the weather without unlocking your computer.

Customization of your Windows 8 lock screen is located in the PC settings portion of your computer. Opening the lock screen settings begins by you first opening Settings and then selecting change PC settings. You can then personalize your lock screen by selecting the category of your interest and clicking lock screen. You may also choose one of the backgrounds or images already present on your computer or camera.

How can you further customize your lock screen widgets? Lock screen widgets often referred to as lock screen apps allow you to view information at a glance. Even if your computer is locked the apps will continue to run in the background and will allow you to access updates that will ultimately be displayed on the lock screen. Your lock screen widgets can be configured the way you would like them to be displayed on your computer.

If your newly customized lock screen is not set to your personal preferences no need to worry there are applications available to enhance your lock screen features far beyond the previously set Windows 8 factory settings. An application known as the Chameleon app is able to watch photo of the day services that will in turn allow you to continuously change your lock screen background on a schedule. Although this is not included with the Windows 8 operating system, the Chameleon app is available at the Windows Store and compatible with Window 8 devices.

Although Window 8 customizations are important because they allow you as a Windows 8 user to set your own personal preferences, upgrades are also of grave significance. An upgrade allows you to install the latest version of a program, which offers you access to more programs.

You do not have to search for upgrades because Windows automatically installs important updates as they become available. However, these preferences can be changed and you can turn automatic updating on or off. Windows updates allow you to choose to have recommended updates automatically installed on your computer or you can be notified when such updates are available. Notification of updates allows you to choose when you would like them installed on the computer rather than having them automatically downloaded. So, keep your computer up to date and running well with Windows 8 upgrades.

Thinking about upgrading your Windows 8 version: windows 8.1 is an update which incorporates more than the already available 800 updates to the Windows 8 operating system. This new update will have the capability to boot directly back to desktop mode with the click of the Start menu. This enables the Start screen to be displayed while in the desktop mode. Apps and other features will be able to be accessed by merely swiping up from the Start menu.

The Windows 8.1 upgrade offers additional features as well. The Windows 8.1 on-screen keyboard allows users to be more productive while writing due to changes that have been made to the auto-suggest feature. Now the auto-suggest feature requires you to simply slide your finger across the spacebar to select the word. Another improved aspect that the Windows 8.1 upgrade offers is the addition of keys. You will now be able to select additional keys without changing pages.

Other customizations and upgrades are currently being developed. Upon implementation of such key features and updates the Windows 8 operating system will be far beyond the best operating system to date. It is therefore essential that you learn how to make changes to Windows 8 by doing customizations and upgrades.

CHAPTER 5- WINDOWS – HOW STORAGE WORKS- THE OPTIONS

For years, the only method of storing data on a computer system was locally. When you saved a data file it simply would go directly to the hard drive or other internal memory system, which in turn would allow you to easily access the files later. However, the hard drive would quickly run out of space, forcing you to venture into the system manager and remove files that are less important to you.

While the larger size of hard drives have made that not as often of an issue, storing all of your data files locally still isn't always the best option. This is why there are now multiple storage methods available on Windows 8, so if you are new to the operating system or if you are just wondering what options you have, each is going to provide you with a desirable method for saving your files.

Local Hard Drive

As covered earlier, the local hard drive is one of the most commonly used methods for storing data. Hard drives are helpful as it is quick and easy to save, although the hard drive space is eventually going to fill up, plus if the hard drive fails on you, you're going to lose all of your information, not to mention it is difficult to transport the information to another computer when necessary.

Removable Storage

Removable storage options have been around for some time, but the method has changed a lot. Floppy disks once reigned supreme with this form of storage, but truth be told floppy disks did not store much data at all. One disk held 1.44 MB worth of data, and nowadays a lot of song downloads wouldn't even fit onto that, let along larger files. Since the floppy disk, Zip disks came along, increasing storage capacity but didn't prove all that practical, and while it is possible to burn data onto a CD or DVD, this is more of a backup method than an option for quick and easy file transfer, especially as you can't easily alter, delete and change the file information.

Now, USB based flash drives make it quick and easy to store data, and these work exceptionally well on Windows 8. The flash drives plug into a USB port and instantly offer multiple, even hundreds, of gigabytes worth of storage instantly. For someone who wants to keep the data local, yet still travel with it, removable storage on Windows 8 computers is a desirable option.

Indexed

Indexed storage options are typically associated with networks. If you work in an office or other facility, your indexed file is going to be saved on the network drive. This gives you the ability to open the files without having to transport the files from one computer to another. While this is still a local based format, it gives you the option of retrieving the information from any of the computers connected to the network. Now, with wireless networks, a laptop or even tablet computer doesn't have to be plug into the network for you to retrieve the files.

As long as you are within range of the network (generally inside the building) you shouldn't have trouble accessing the files stored on it. Of course, should you want to take the data files and move the information to a different computer not found on the network, it is necessary to save the files on an external device, such as a USB flash drive, and move it to the other computer unless you have access to the next method of storage on Windows 8 computers.

Remote

A remote based storage option is also known as a cloud service. Windows uses Azure SkyDrive, although there are other cloud services offered by Google and Apple (many of the different cloud services are actually maintained by Microsoft and other, single companies though). A cloud service allows you to instantly save your information to a remote based hard drive through an Internet connection. Chances are you will never come in contact with this hard drive, or ever see it, as it is stored in a large facility with trillions upon trillions of other GB worth of storage space. By saving the information on your Windows 8 computer through the remote cloud service, you are able to access the information on any other computer in the world, as long as there is an Internet connection present.

The cloud service works in a very similar way as your email account. You have a log in username and password, which is required to enter into your account. Once the necessary information is input into the service, you are able to view all of the files you have uploaded to the cloud service. While viewing, these files stay on the cloud, so it is not necessary to download any of the content. However, should you want the files to be stored locally on your other computer; you only need to select the file and have it downloaded to your computer. The same process takes place when you upload the files to the cloud service. Either way, as long as there is an Internet connection present, you always have access to the remote cloud based files you saved with Windows 8.

The new Windows 8 operating system has several different storage options available to you. Windows the internal, locally saved hard drive is always a valuable option for some computer specific files, there are many times where you want to take the files with you to a different computer. Removable storage devices, indexed storage options and remote cloud services are all extremely valuable, so the next time you are looking at saving a file on your computer, you just need to know what options you have available. This way, you can save the files to your computer, to the cloud or anywhere else, and you'll have access to the files at a later date. This is just one of the many improvements made on Windows 8 that are not found in previous versions.

CHAPTER 6- HOW TO CREATE & EDIT MOVIES, PHOTOS AND MUSIC

Movies

There are a number of ways that you can create and edit videos using Windows 8, but Windows Movie Maker 2012—formerly Windows Live Movie Maker—is by far the most popular video editing tool used by Windows 8 PC owners.

The program has a very simplistic interface. It opens to a white screen in which you can drag and drop photos, videos and music. Users can add as many clips as they would like to. Once the clips are added, the clearly defined tabs can be used to perform different types of editing. The basic tabs are Home, Animations, Visual Effects, View and Edit. The tab section can be expanded into additional categories depending upon any additional features that might be needed.

The Home tab allows users to take new photos and videos on demand with the computer's webcam. It also includes basic editing tools (crop, rotate, delete) and an "Auto Movie Theme" section where Windows has created preset movie themes and animations for users to implement.

The Animations tab is used to create video and picture effects, and animated transitions between clips.

The Visual Effects tab allows users to alter or dramatize images and video clips completely. Users could, for example, invert the colors of a clip or give it a cartoonish look.

The View tab gives users the ability to view their videos in intricate detail. With this tab, a user can zoom in or out of a video and preview it full screen.

The Edit tab, which is a part of the expandable video tools section, has options to crossfade and trim audio/video clips.

For advanced users, the Video Tools section can be expanded for additional features.

Once a video has been created, Windows gives users the option to burn the video to a disc, save it as a project or save it as a video file.

If Windows Movie Maker 2012 is not preloaded on your Windows 8 computer, it can be downloaded here for free.

A snapshot of the Windows Movie Maker 2012 interface can be seen below:

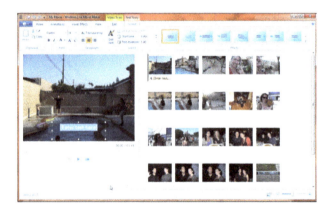

Photos

Windows 8 users have the benefit of two photo editing programs: Paint and Windows Photo Gallery—formerly Windows Live Photo Gallery.

Jason Scotts

Windows Photo Gallery

This program is the simpler, more intuitive of the two stock photo editing programs for Windows 8. It includes five tabs, which are as follows: Home, Edit, Find, Create and View.

The primary function of the Home tab is image searching capability. It also allows users to tag people in photos via the Windows Live network and create slideshows.

The Edit tab has basic photo editing features. Here users can adjust photo exposure, color levels, noise levels, crop, rotate and add effects to images. It also includes an auto adjust button for quick enhancement of photos.

The Find tab provides users with advanced searching capabilities. Users can search by date, quality rating, file type and user tags with the buttons in the Find tab.

With the Create tab users are able to use multiple photos to create something new. It includes features that give users the power to fuse photos, create collages and post to blogs. Advanced users can download additional tools to broaden the Create tab's functionality.

The Windows Photo Gallery View tab has the most advanced set of viewing features of any stock Windows media editing program. Users can zoom, view slideshows, view multiple images, flag photos, rate photos, view multiple photos at once and add captions.

If Windows Photo Gallery is not preloaded on your Windows 8 computer, it can be downloaded here for free.

A snapshot of the Windows Photo Gallery interface can be seen below:

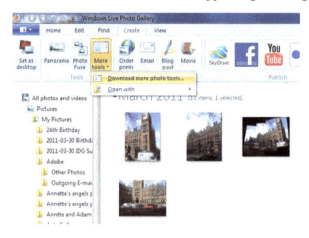

Paint

With only two tabs, it can appear simple at first, but Paint is actually for users with advanced PC sketching and editing skills. The two tabs, which are described in detail below, are Home and View.

The Home tab is where all of the essential editing functions are located. Inside of this tab are seven sub-tabs. They are as follows:

Clipboard- This provides access to the cut, copy and paste tools.

Image- The Image sub-tab allows users to rotate, resize, crop and make area selections within the image.

Brushes- This sub-tab is where the primary drawing tools are located. It has a number of brush options to select for drawing.

Shapes- With the shapes sub-tab users are enabled to create predefined shapes, lines and curves.

Size- The buttons in the Size sub-tab allow users to alter the thickness of the lines of their brush strokes and shapes.

Colors- Here users can select colors from a predefined list; they can also use a color spectrum palette to create custom colors.

The View tab allows users to view images full screen, zoom and add assistive gridlines for their sketches.

Although these tools are primarily used for creating drawings from scratch, skilled users can use them for advanced photo editing.

Paint should come preloaded on every Windows 8 PC. If it is not and you would like to use it, immediately contact Windows customer support.

A snapshot of the Paint interface can be seen below:

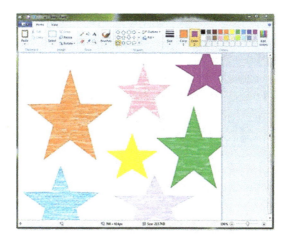

Music

Although Windows 8 does not come preloaded with any useful music editing tools, there are several available for download. Due to its ease of use and free license, Audacity is the most popular of all of the music editing programs for Windows 8.

Audacity's primary editing features are in a large toolbar right below its tabs. Right below the toolbar, the primary interface allows users to play, edit and fuse multiple audio samples. They even provide a visual depiction of the wavelengths that compose the sounds of each sample, which adds a visual element to the editing process. The tabs above the primary editing functions allow users to access files, create effects, access advanced editing features and transform projects into media tracks.

Audacity can be downloaded to your Windows 8 computer here for free.

A snapshot of the Audacity interface can be viewed below:

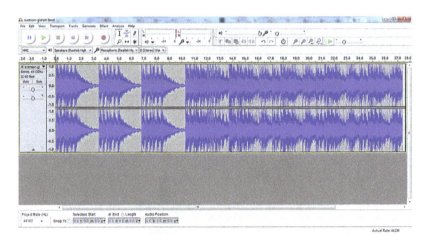

CHAPTER 7- HOW TO FIND LOST FILES IN WINDOWS 8

With so many files on your computer system, it is incredibly easy to lose track of some of these files and to eventually not even know where the files are saved. Whether the files have just been misplaced or actually deleted, it is possible locate and recover the lost files in Windows 8. There are several different features available to you in order to do just this, which is why you need to take advantage of every opportunity you have. There is nothing worse than losing a file, and you need to know how to obtain this information in order to locate it and avoid having to recreate the information again.

For starters, you are able to look for the file using the search folder in Windows 8. To do this, open the search window by pressing the Windows logo key and F at the same time. Once the search window is up you can type in the name of the file, or at least part of the name, as long as you can remember it. If you can't remember this but know a tag the file was using, you can type hit into the search field in order to reduce the number of returned possible options.

If you were not able to retrieve any information through the Search window option, you can look for the file in the folder it is most likely going to be. This gives you a few different options to check for the file, and each method for searching for the file is going to be helpful for different kinds of files, ranging from word processor documents to images.

If you want to retrieve a world processor document, select the "Start" button and choose "Documents." This brings up the documents folder and any other document saved into the folder. Of course, if you changed the save location it is not going to be in here, but if you didn't alter any of the factory settings, than you shouldn't have a problem locating the content right here.

If, however, you are looking for a picture, you need to click the "Start" button and then choose "Pictures." This is going to bring up a new window with all of the pictures stored on your computer. While you might have to flip through a few different pictures in order to locate the one you are searching for, this is a valuable option and one that you need to consider when searching for the information.

The Recycle Bin is one that is going to be a good location to search. The Recycle Bin can be opened by double-clicking the Recycle Bin icon on the desktop. This shows all of the files that have been removed from the computer but remain attached, just in case you want to reinstall the content later. When you delete a file it ends up in the Recycle Bin as a safety net. It is not going to be removed from the Recycle Bin until you clear the bin out. However, if you do locate the file inside the bin you need to select it and choose "Restore" in order to restore it back to the original location. This information will be displayed, so you know where it is located. You can also just click and drag the file to any desired location on the desktop or computer window, should you want to change where it is being saved.

You might also want to check the default save location of the program you used to create and edit the file. In order to do this you need to load the program you used to save and produce the file. One the software is running you need to click "File" in the menu, and then select "Save As." this opens the default save location and is going to show you all of the other files that are currently saved. Once you know what the default save location is you can go about trying to locate the file in this window. if it is still not there, then it might mean you have deleted from the hard drive. However, even if the file has been deleted from the hard drive it doesn't necessarily mean it is no longer possible to retrieve and recover. In fact, as long as you haven't saved over or added new programming hardware and software to the computer, you should still be able to locate the file.

In order to locate a file that has been deleted from the hard drive you need to install a retrieval computer program. This software is going to scan your hard drive not only for files saved on the computer, but also files that have been deleted but still remain on the drive. While the files do not appear in the search features, the remnants of the file are still stored on the computer. As long as new, large programs have not been added and saved over the place of the previously stored file on the hard drive, then you should be able to retrieve the file and get it back. To do this, open the retrieval program that you want to use. There are dozens available through the application stores and even for free through multiple download websites on the Internet.

With the software open you just need to tell it to start scanning your hard drive for any possible files that it can recover. Depending on the size of your hard drive, the available space left on the hard drive and the amount of files it is scanning over, this process can take anywhere from a few minutes to several hours. Once the scan has finished you are able to view all of the possible files that can be recovered. If you notice the file you want then you just need to click on the file and choose the "Recover" feature in the program. While the exact method of retrieving the file is different, depending on the program you use and the version it is, once the file has been retrieved you can use it like new.

CHAPTER 8- THE ART OF PRINTING FROM WINDOWS 8

Windows 8 has been designed to make sure that the user can use different styles of print techniques. When printing with Windows 8 you, the user can customize the document in many different ways. They can change the paper size, the way the document is laid out on the paper, and all of this can be done by using very simple and easy key functions on the key board.

Even if the user does not want to customize their work in the print system, Windows 8 provides the user with many unique features when they are trying to print. The default features of the print system of Windows 8 are very unique and are not the same as any other computer system.

If the user is using the printer driver model V3 with Windows 8, the printer driver will continue to work, even though it was developed before Windows 8. When the user wants to print from a store bought device to the printer, the user will be met with the set printing options. The default printing options have many different futures including paper size, format, and making duplicates of the same document. All these features are usable on many different printer types. There is one down fall to using the V3 printer driver with Windows 8, that is that, the pin secured printing option is not available.

The printer driver model (V4) has been revamped to work with Windows 8. Incorporated into the printer driver (V4) is the desk top apps and the windows store apps. The V4 printer device has an extension known as the printer extension. The printer extension will provide the user with custom print preferences. This driver model can also provide the user with the essential printer notifications.

When a user hooks up a device to a computer which has Windows 8, the computer will automatically search for the best drivers to run the device. The computer will automatically download the best drivers for the device you are trying to run, so that your device will run efficiently, this includes a printer.

Users can customize the print system in Windows 8 more than they could have in any other Windows system. Windows 8 is the most versatile system that is on the market to be able to run any kind of device that can be hooked up to the computer. Printers are a breeze to hook up to a computer and get working very quickly. From the very first time a printer is hooked up to the computer it will give you a screen that the user can customize very easily to fit their needs.

The Windows store app can be configured to help extend the printer settings that are available on Windows 8. When the user starts up the printer, they can be notified that the ink is running low in the printer. When the ink is low it can affect your printing ability and ruin the printing your doing. The user will want to know when the ink is low before starting the printing so that their paper does not get ruined. The printer will also be able to tell you if you have a paper jam.

The printing ability with Windows 8 can give each user creative scenarios to work with and find different ways to print out the document that needs to be printed out.

Windows 8 desktop offers many different ways to print a paper, offers much more control to the user than any other Windows system. To start off with the user will need to choose print from the program files menu, next the user will want to click on the programs print icon, this icon is usually labeled as a picture of a tiny printer. The user can also click on the print button on the programs tool bar.

As you can tell printing with Windows 8 can be very versatile and rewarding. There are many different ways to print using this Windows system, and any type of experienced user can find a way that will surely work for them when trying to print a document. After selecting a way to print the document, you will need to click the word print that comes up in the dialogue box. Once you click on the word print then your document will start printing.

If the user would rather not go through a lot of steps at one time to get a document printed then simply add a "print" short cut to the desk to itself. By having a short cut on the desk top printing any documents will be able to be printed easily.

The one important thing to remember about printing when using Windows 8 is that, Windows 8 is more modern and if you are used to the old way of printing a document, then you may need to read up on how to print using Windows 8 because it is way different than any other Windows on the market today. Printing is the same on the desk top applications so you will not have to learn anything new when trying to print off the desk top applications. If you choose to download a modern app, then you will have to print by using a charm bar on the desk top.

Windows 8 has many different support systems that will allow you to print by using many different types of printers but will support fewer drivers. BY using less drivers, you will be reducing the amount of disk space that used on the computer itself and your computer will be open so the user can down load more games and have more speed on the computer.

Overall printing with Windows 8 is much more versatile and much easier for the user in the long run. Once the user learns how to use the printer options in Windows 8, the user will not want to go back and use any other Windows to print with. The user will learn to love the printing options in Windows 8.

ABOUT THE AUTHOR

Jason Scotts has always loved the fact that software can make doing things so much easier and thus consume less time. However, feeling intimidated by what it can do and how to use it stopped him from allowing software to save that precious time of his. He found himself asking all his friends if they can show him how to use certain software that he just couldn't grasp. Bothering them about it all the time made him feel like a nuisance. So finally, he set a goal for himself, no matter what it took, to learn everything he could about using particularly Windows 8.

After personally using it every single day and challenging himself to use aspects of it that he didn't even need but just wanted to know how it's done lead him to knowing more about it than he ever thought he could. Eventually, it started to become easier for him and the intimidation just went away. So from personal experience and the confidence he's built up, he felt it was time to put it in writing so that others who have a hard time with this can benefit and be on their way to enjoying the use of great software.